10 Steps to Overcome Divorce Stress

10 Steps to Overcome Divorce Stress

experienced and shared by

PATRICIA A MULLINS

Purpose Publishing Purpose Publishing

13194 US Highway 301 S #417

Riverview, FL 33578

ISBN-13: 978-1-965319-11-6 paperback
ISBN-13: 978-1-965319-18-5 (eBook)

Printed in the United States of America.

I chose ten steps because of the Biblical meaning of the number.

Ten represents divine laws: righteousness, responsibility, perfection, judgment, and completeness.

Ten follows nine, the number of spiritual completion, signifying that the spiritually complete man or woman walks full of God's power, authority, and righteousness.

Daffodils are some of the first flowers we see in springtime and are a great indicator that winter is over.

Because of this, they are seen to represent rebirth and new beginnings.

Daffodils represent inspiration, awareness, inner reflection, forgiveness, and vitality.

I hope that you strive to become more like the daffodil.

Sincerely, Patricia

CONTENTS

BOOK REVIEWS

The contents of this book help extinguish the fire in the stressors of divorce, and it will surely help others meet these ten stressors and challenges and move on in life. It is an excellent read and opens the door to stressors that are not easily understood or discussed. Patricia is passionate, caring, and committed, and she has shown mercy by expounding on her experience so that she can help others. I recognize these steps, which help me to share what others may be thinking; they allow for introspection and teach me how to move forward from hurtful experiences. The stress and experience do not get easier... but this book reminds one that one gets stronger with God's wisdom, strength, and comfort, which makes the stressors seem more manageable. I think the readers of this book will grow to understand their experiences better and to appreciate how to move forward with their lives. Some steps are familiar, hard to understand, and communicate when you do not recognize your relationship or yourself. Divorce hurts many people, and hopefully, this book will help to seal the hole in the divorce moneybags and make recovery more accessible.

Anonymous, divorced three times, Melbourne, Florida.

This guidebook serves as a roadmap to the emotional housekeeping necessary to navigate the challenges that can cause stress during divorce. It walks the reader through practical steps to manage their emotions and move forward despite the pain divorce can cause. It offers positive affirmations and scriptures to support the reader's healing journey. Through introspection and reflection, the reader is encouraged to take responsibility for managing their emotions and is given tools to build a reimagined inner framework of self-love, acceptance, forgiveness, and hope for a future as a healed and whole individual.

To move the reader through the healing process from the inside out, Patricia serves as a coach who is vulnerable and transparent about her own divorce experience and proves that moving forward is possible with consistent intentionality and the courage to do the work. Change is hard, but this guidebook offers tools to navigate the unknown. The content highlights the ten essential steps and is insightful and encouraging, supporting the much-needed community. The vocabulary is conversational, making it an easy read. I appreciate the practical steps, the wealth of scripture, and the abundance of positive affirmations provided for each of the ten steps, which all help build confidence and provide strength along the way.

Because the divorce journey can be daunting and very lonely, often riddled with unanswered questions and overwhelming with self-doubt, the reader can use this guidebook as a quick and handy reference to combat these and any other unpredictable negative thoughts or feelings that often try to keep the reader emotionally debilitated. I see this as a powerful weapon in the fight against emotional bankruptcy. Rooted in faith, Patricia provides a pathway to transformative growth, and this guidebook can be essential for anyone experiencing divorce.

Sandi is enjoying singlehood again. Chicago, IL.

Patricia has put together a solid guide to help those who are going through or have experienced the divorce process. Through her experience, she helps the reader navigate everyday stressors, thoughts, and feelings associated with the trauma of divorce. Her perspective and biblical passages give hope and confirmation that no one is alone at any point in their journey. I particularly like how she couples scripture with therapy references. We suffer in silence when dealing with issues because we are ashamed or do not want to burden others with our experiences. I wish I had a guidebook like this to refer to when I was going through my divorce; it could have helped me navigate my negative thinking.

Mary recently divorced and is dating again. Palm Bay, FL.

The book speaks volumes regarding the stresses experienced during divorce and the outcome, including overcoming bitterness and unforgiveness. WOW!!! I do not know where to start; the book is impressive. While reading some parts, I became angry because I did not allow *myself* to heal and forgive. This makes me feel as though I held a lot of bitterness, frustration, anger, and emotions that caused so many difficult areas in my life. I also read parts of the book and realized I may not be healed after five years. That is where the emotional house cleaning comes in.

Sam divorced and cautiously dating. Montgomery, AL.

Patt embodies optimism. She pours her heart into this book to show us how to do our work so that we can realize that a loving and purposeful God fearfully and wonderfully made us. Take the time necessary to invest in yourself by applying these words of wisdom from an overcomer of deep pain and disappointment. This book is about empowerment. Patt permits us to show up for ourselves, love, and prioritize our health and well-being. Your tomorrow is waiting for you.

Donna is happily single and traveling the globe. Olympia Fields, IL.

FOREWORD

My relationship with Patt goes back to 1990, when I was introduced to her through a mutual male friend I later married. She was not just a friend but also my maid of honor. Little did I know then that we would share a common experience.

I was divorced years before Patt in 1988. I was unaware of any resources that could have helped my healing process from a biblical standpoint. I was offered medications for anger and depression, but nothing to address the emotions I was overcome by.

Patt's guidebook discusses emotional house cleaning and forgiveness as essential steps for moving forward from a divorce. However, she shares her journey, making her advice more than just book knowledge; it is a life-changing experience. I happened to be one of the friends who witnessed Patt go through her divorce, but I did not see the battles she had fought when she went home to her home. One can say that she fought battles so others could have a battle plan.

Mrs. Anna Hannah, nurse and wife of John F. Hannah, New Life Covenant Church Southeast. Chicago, Illinois

With great enthusiasm, I write this foreword for Patricia Mullins' latest work - 10 Steps to Overcome Divorce Stress.

As an executive pastor who has witnessed the multifaceted challenges individuals face navigating the turbulent waters of divorce, I attest to the book's immense value.

The journey through divorce is rarely linear; it is a complex interchange of grief, confusion, and adjustment. Patricia Mullins's compassionate and biblical approach offers a guiding light for those grappling with these difficulties.

This book is a testament to Patricia Mullins' dedication to helping others find peace and strength during life's challenges. It is an invaluable resource for anyone struggling with the ongoing challenges of divorce. I wholeheartedly recommend 10 Steps to Overcome Divorce Stress to you, trusting that it will serve as a profound source of comfort and direction on your journey toward healing.

Will Price, husband and Executive Pastor, Calvary Church, Port St. Lucie, Florida.

HOW TO READ THIS GUIDEBOOK?

Before you turn another page, you must know how to read this book, which should be read as a guide. Take a moment to pray before you start reading and ask God for clarity so that you can understand how to apply each step to your life.

Each step in the book is a crucial action towards healing and wholeness. Some steps might feel uncomfortable, unfamiliar, or hard to grasp, but your active participation is critical. So, reread them with an open mind and without judgment.

Take notes if you need to. Read every affirmation and scripture aloud, no matter how awkward it feels, especially when I suggest you stand in front of a mirror. Accept that you might experience a breakdown before you get a breakthrough.

As you begin this transformational journey, make a firm commitment to yourself. Promise that you will start and finish this book, and if necessary, read it as often as needed. Your dedication will be the key to unlocking the healing and wholeness you seek.

Your journey partner,
Patricia

Emotional House Cleaning

I was in my late thirties when I contemplated divorcing my husband after two and a half years of marriage. My wedding planner introduced me to Emotional House Cleaning (EHC), and I was intrigued to learn more about the subject. Suggesting that I start with a clean emotional slate, she advised that I begin the divorce procedures by visually and emotionally detaching myself from being a wife and a bonus mom to my stepson. I stood in the living room alone and cried to God to help me start my healing process.

I was blessed to have a great support system of believers who only wanted what was best for me. Those brothers and sisters in the faith assured me that I was not alone. Coming to terms with ending my marriage was not an easy decision, but it was the best choice for me. Let us learn a little more about how to apply Emotional House Cleaning.

The EHC exercise can shorten your healing process if you give yourself time. Trust me, EHC is never pretty or easy to manage. Just note that, with God by your side and this guidebook in your hands, you will find tools and exercises to walk you through what may feel like walking through the valley of death. The good news is that EHC is highly effective when you allow yourself time for healing as raw emotions surface.

What exactly is Emotional House Cleaning? EHC brings awareness to your emotional and mental health as you go through a highly stressful process. You can expect to feel sad, angry, exhausted, lonely, frustrated, and confused—and you will express these feelings at the most awkward moments. You will feel anxious about your future and the unknown. So, beware that your emotions and reactions to them will intensify and take you on a wild emotional roller coaster ride.

Some of these emotions will look like brokenness, denial, sadness, loneliness, anger, depression, thoughts of defeat, loss, confusion, etc. Make sure you have a box of tissues because you will need it. I have added note pages at the back of the book, a place, so that you can write down your feelings and identify which emotions reoccur repeatedly.

I promise you that you will be on your road to releasing those negative thoughts and emotions.

Now, let us get started. Stand before a full-length mirror and release the first emotion that overwhelms you. Say these affirmations and scriptures at the end of the chapter at least 2-5 times each, for at least 5 to 10 minutes, repeating them daily (you may add your own choice of scripture).

AFFIRMATIONS:

- I clear all the ways I feel I have been deceived.
- I release all the tension and pain of holding on too tightly.
- I am open to new possibilities for my future, which I cannot yet imagine.
- Everything that is not meant for my highest good must leave.
- Just because it did not work out does not mean my life is over.
- Even though I may miss some things about my ex-spouse and my relationship, I am happier and healthier being single.
- As a lesson learned, every experience is perfect for my growth.
- Every part of me is getting the optimum benefit from this exercise.

- God is leading me to a place of health and wholeness.

I'm sure it's safe to say that I have found myself in a place of loneliness, sadness, happiness, and sensitivity all at once—and so will you. All my emotions were coming at me simultaneously, and I was unsure how or what I should feel. But, again, I was ready to start the emotional house-cleaning process. I was committed to taking control of my emotions and actions. I knew I needed to take control of myself and focus on the inner me... and this was where emotional housekeeping came in.

Unknowingly, I developed some intentional habits that saved my life within the first month of leaving the marriage. Below are some of the steps of EHC that I am sure you will find helpful on your road to recovery. Ask yourself these questions:

1. **Do I hear what is going on internally?**
   Start by tuning into your emotional self. Imagine your body as the radio and the stations as your emotions. During the day, you may be tuned into different stations depending on your thoughts and feelings. You need to identify those emotions and find out what is triggering them by making sure you tune into them. You must feel it to heal it!

2. **Do you know what your triggers are?**
   Anger and depression are recognized signals. We cannot become upset or annoyed about something we are unaware of. So, both anger and depression signal you to think about and identify the triggers. You need to recognize your emotional triggers.

3. **When was the last time you looked under your rug?**

   Sometimes, in my relationships with my ex-husband, family, close friends, or even co-workers, I wanted to say something but did not. This could be about what I was thinking or how I was feeling. What happens to those thoughts and feelings is that they get pushed under the rug. With time, more thoughts and emotions get pushed under the metaphorical carpet, and they start to build up until one day, they explode and make a big, fat mess. You must avoid this at all costs. When I have conversations with those important to me, I ensure my approach is led honestly. Now, these chats are honest and not passive-aggressive or filled with a blaming tone. This novel approach took a lot out of me, and it still does. However, I was determined to speak with integrity.

4. **Are you quick to judge?**

   I remember a friend advising me to stop the judgment chatter about my ex. It knocked me off my feet, but I was not offended because I knew she was right. That day, I began to practice the idea that if I did not have anything good to say about him, then I would not say anything at all. Remember, we all have good days and bad days. What is essential here is to allow yourself some freedom to have those random feelings—good or bad—with no cause or reason. You should not be too quick to judge your feelings. If something needs your attention, your emotions will persist. Do not let judgment or intrusive thoughts overtake you.

5. **Do you know what is emotionally draining you?**
   Ask yourself this question: what am I doing that is draining my life? You need to know what is draining you—in other words, what is keeping you up at night, making you sensitive, or causing worry. Think about the situations you are in, or even better, the people you surround yourself with regularly. How do you feel when you are with them? Do you feel drained, sad, insecure, or belittled after spending time with them? If so, get that drain cleaner out and unblock these emotions. Take control of how, where, when, and with whom you spend your valuable time. Once time is gone, you never get it back!

6. **What more do you need?**
   Once you know the trigger and have unblocked your drain, figure out what you need more of in your life. Get a pen and paper, and list at least ten things you want more of. There are no right or wrong answers here because this is about YOU. I realized I needed time to myself doing what I enjoy! So, I set aside a few hours weekly to spend time in Bible study, kickboxing, dancing, and walking, which I found enjoyable and revitalizing. Once I got home, I felt recharged. These emotional house-cleaning steps improved my well-being, actively creating the life I wanted—and you can do it, too.

7. **Can you identify who your loyal friends are?**
   Take a minute to reflect on the close friends and acquaintances you have in your life. A close friend is someone I have mutual affection for, someone I can trust and value their opinion. After not speaking to them for months, I realized they were also

people I could pick up with right where I left off. They do not judge me. I will go out of my way to schedule time with them, even if it is just a quick chat, text, or phone catch-up.

It would be best if you had a friend who speaks about life and encourages you. If they do not, find another friend who will.

8. **Can you find something to be grateful for in your divorce process?**
   I am sure you have heard about gratitude journals and their benefits. Take a step back, be grateful for what you have, and stop thinking or chasing after what you do not have. This took me some time to understand, but once I started appreciating the good in my life—even on my worst days—there was always something I could be grateful for. Practice daily reading of encouraging affirmations that will build up your fragile emotions.

So, there you have it. We all have areas that need work, but awareness matters most. There is no judgment here. Being dragged down and feeling overwhelmed with emotions does not add balance to your life, and an unbalanced life is an unstable life when trying to live happy, healthy, and whole. We can all do some emotional house cleaning. Remember this:

Emotions dictate how we feel and think, and they are at the heart of achieving what we want.

SCRIPTURES:

- *Are you weary, carrying a heavy burden? Then come to me. I will refresh your life, for I am your oasis. Join your life with mine. Learn my ways, and you will discover that I am gentle, humble, and easy to please. You will find refreshment and rest in me. All that I require of you will be pleasant and easy to bear* (Matthew 11:28-30, The Passion Translation TPT).

- *Stop dwelling on the past. I do not even remember these former things. I am doing something brand new, something unheard of. Even now, it sprouts, grows, and matures. Don't you perceive it? I will make a way in the wilderness and open flowing streams in the desert* (Isaiah 43:18-19, TPT).

- *Though all your wanderings wearied you, you never said, "I give up." Your strength was renewed, so you never fainted* (Isaiah 57:10, TPT).

- *There is no broken heart and no situation too messy for His love. The God who hung the stars will strengthen you and hold you together* (Psalm 147:3-6, TPT).

Our strength grows out of our weaknesses.
— *Ralph Waldo Emerson*

Practice Forgiveness

What is forgiveness precisely, and how do you forgive someone? I am glad you asked. Forgiveness is a conscious, deliberate decision to release feelings of resentment or revenge toward a person or group who has harmed you, whether or not forgiveness is deserved. However, it is essential to remember that forgiveness does not mean forgetting or excusing past offenses. You choose to let go of the bitterness, resentment, and anger.

Forgiveness is one of the most misunderstood concepts, yet people often express clichés such as "forgive and forget" as if it is an effortless process. However, the importance of forgiveness takes on a new meaning after divorce. No one marries with the intent of divorcing, so hurt and shame can run deep.

Sometimes, people equate forgiveness with weakness, and it is also widely believed that if you forgive someone, you condone their behavior. In my case, I held a grudge against my ex-husband for the first year or so and was unable to forgive him for his part in our divorce. Unforgiveness was easier to manage because it was a familiar emotion, whereas forgiveness made me feel vulnerable. However, I now realize that forgiveness breeds freedom.

Forgiving others is terrifying yet necessary for healthy relationships. It is about being willing to acknowledge that you are capable of being wounded and able to risk exposing yourself. It also means stepping out of the role of a victim and taking charge of your life. I did not always practice forgiveness as God commanded of me. I was broken, hurt, and confused once I decided divorce was the path I was going to take. So, as I took the first step to file and began the procedures, I knew my emotions would go haywire. Then I realized that all those negative emotions had to be wrangled with. There was, indeed, a spiritual warfare in the making. I began to practice forgiveness for my soon-to-be ex-husband and myself.

At this point, forgiveness was a touchy concept for me, but I was also wise enough to know that it was a command-ment I was mandated to practice as a Christian. Thank God for the principles in these Bible verses that can help you choose to follow God, no matter how unhappy you may feel when considering divorce. When you obey God despite your circumstances, you can find peace and hope to carry you through. Practicing forgiveness is not a suggestion but a command from Jesus, as stated in Luke 17:3 (NIV): *"If your brother or sister sins against you, rebuke them; and if they repent, forgive them."*

Now, let us get started. Stand before a full-length mirror and release the first emotion that overwhelms you. Say these affirmations and scriptures at the end of the chapter at least 2-5 times each for 5 to 10 minutes, repeating them daily. *(You may add your own choice of scriptures.)*

AFFIRMATIONS:

- I will develop a forgiving heart and forgive often.
- I forgive myself for the hurt I am experiencing.
- I forgive my ex.
- I release all these unrelenting, painful thoughts and emotions.
- I choose to let go because I cannot control anyone but myself.
- I release all fears of not being perfect.
- I release grief.
- I let go of past regrets, and I release the past.
- I release all the ways I feel responsible.

- I release all these feelings of being sick to my stomach.
- I choose to release anger, hurt, and negative self-talk.
- I am entirely expected to be upset or devastated by this breakup.
- It is okay to think about my ex-spouse, question what happened, and replay every detail in my head. But eventually, I will move on!
- Every heartbreak is a lesson learned.
- I release regret from every aspect of my life because it serves me no good.

The following pages are from 'What to Do When You Feel Stuck in an Unhappy Marriage' - Bothell Christian Counseling.

Here are a few helpful verses you can refer to when you need encouragement and hope.

Remember that spiritual battles are ongoing.

You have a spiritual enemy, Satan, who has done everything he can to destroy your marriage. He has planted seeds of discontent, grumbling, criticism, and more to disrupt the unity between you and your spouse. These seeds will sprout into ongoing spiritual battles that may look like arguments or withdrawal between you and your spouse on the surface.

But you can fight back with the principles in Ephesians 6:11-18 (NLT):

11. *"Put on all of God's armor so that you will be able to stand firm against all strategies of the devil."*

12. *For we are not fighting against flesh-and-blood enemies, but against evil rulers and authorities of the unseen world, against mighty powers in this dark world, and evil spirits in the heavenly places.*
13. *Therefore, put on every piece of God's armor so you will be able to resist the enemy in the time of evil. Then, after the battle, you will still be standing firm.*
14. *Stand your ground, putting on the belt of truth and the body armor of God's righteousness.*
15. *For shoes, put on the peace that comes from the Good News so that you will be fully prepared.*
16. *In addition to all these, hold up the shield of faith to stop the fiery arrows of the devil.*
17. *Put on salvation as your helmet, and take the sword of the Spirit, which is the Word of God.*
18. *Pray in the Spirit at all times and on every occasion. Stay alert and be persistent in your prayers for all believers everywhere.*

When unhappiness and sadness have overwhelmed you, turn to this passage and ask God for help. He will give you the spiritual tools to fight back and reclaim your commitment to your marriage or your decision to proceed with a divorce.

Protect your heart against temptation.

> *"Keep your heart with all vigilance, for the springs of life flow from it"* (Proverbs 4:23, NLT).

In an unhappy marriage, Satan will tempt you to go astray with many things. You may be drawn to other people who attract you. Romance novels, movies, music, or pornography may even entice you to think other situations would be better for you. These are typical dynamics when couples are unhappy. However, you have the responsibility to guard your heart. When you constantly focus on your divorce, your heart will be discouraged and more open to temptation. But you can identify and cover your weak spots with prayer and by using the steps provided in this guidebook, along with the assistance of a well-trained (Christian) counselor.

Make prayer a high priority.

> "Rejoicing in hope; patient in tribulation; continuing steadfastly in prayer" (Romans 12:12, ASV).

You can turn to God in prayer every time you feel unhappy with your divorce. Pour out all your feelings because He can handle all of them. He will affirm you and strengthen you even when you are struggling. You can ask Him to guide your thoughts, words, and actions toward your ex-spouse. You can also rejoice in the confident hope that God is available to help you at all times of the day. Ask God to give you patience in your divorce troubles, and do not stop praying no matter how you feel.

Always choose to express love.

> "Love bears all things, believes all things, hopes all things, endures all things" (1 Corinthians 13:7, CEB).

It only takes one person to change an unhappy marriage. However, if you are reading this guidebook, you are likely in the divorce process or divorced. You can still be loving toward your ex-spouse, no matter how they treat you. Your commitment, faith, hope, and endurance will serve as an excellent example of grace displayed.

Gratitude is an attitude.

> *"Give thanks in all circumstances, for this is the will of God in Christ Jesus for you"* (1 Thessalonians 5:18, NIV).

You will find it painful to be thankful for your unhappy feelings. However, God desires you to be grateful in all circumstances, even through a divorce. Your gratitude can be based on God's unchanging character, an anchor for your thoughts and feelings. Use the note pages at the back of the book, it is your place to capture and jot down the good things you are thankful for daily. This practice has been proven to uplift one's attitude, so why not try it?

Be responsible for your actions.

> *"Search me, O God, and know my heart! Try me and know my thoughts! And see if there be any wicked way in me, and lead me in the way everlasting."* (Psalm 139:23-24, KJV).

All of us have made mistakes in our marriages that contributed to divorce. You can ask God to search and test you, pointing out anything offensive toward your ex-spouse. He will gently correct you and show you your responsibility in the matter. You may need to confess your sins to your spouse or ex-spouse, which can bring healing and wholeness within and after the divorce procedures. God will reward you for having a humble and teachable spirit.

Forgiveness is a mandate.

> *"Then Peter came up and said to him, 'Lord, how often will my brother sin against me, and I forgive him?"*

"As many as seven times?" Jesus told him, "I do not say to you seven times, but seventy-seven times" (Matthew 18:21-22, NIV).

Your unhappiness may be linked to unforgiveness. When you choose to forgive your ex-spouse not just once but over and over, your feelings will change. Forgiveness is trusting God to handle the problem better than you can. It is an act of surrender and trust in God. It also softens your heart toward your ex-spouse and helps you show greater compassion and love.

SCRIPTURES:

- *Be kind and compassionate to one another, forgiving each other, just as in Christ, God forgave you* (Ephesians 4:32, KJV).

- *For if you forgive other people when they sin against you, your heavenly Father will also forgive you* (Matthew 6:14, KJV).

- *Bear with each other and forgive one another if any of you has a grievance against someone. Forgive as the Lord forgave you* (Colossians 3:13, KJV).

- *Blessed is the one whose transgressions are forgiven, whose sins are covered* (Psalm 32:1, KJV).

- *If we confess our sins, He is faithful and just to forgive us our sins and cleanse us from all unrighteousness* (1 John 1:9, KJV).

Forgiveness is to set a prisoner free and discover that the prisoner was you — *Lewis Smedes*

Love is
Self-Worth

The great vocalist Whitney Houston sings passionately, *"learning to love yourself is the greatest love of all."* Loving yourself first is the best way to start the journey of self-love. I'm a firm believer that self-love is a byproduct of God's love. You owe it to yourself to acknowledge that you are worthy of love. Speak affirmations of kindness, beauty, joy, and compassion to yourself. Practicing self-love is a spiritual journey that requires active participation. It is a path to continuous growth that builds confidence and healing.

Let us pause to reflect on this scripture. What does it mean when Jesus takes time to instruct us about a troubled heart? He says, *"Let not your heart be troubled. Believe in God; believe also in me"* (John 14:1, AMP). It is interesting how Jesus phrased the command, *"Let not your heart be troubled."* He did not simply ask His disciples to try and avoid being fearful or anxious. The fact that He tells them to avoid allowing their hearts to be troubled is evidence that we have control over how we respond to the burdens of life. I understand that we have active participation in how we choose to deal—or not deal—with a broken heart, depression, hurt, anxiety, and grief.

At this stage of your new singleness, restoring your mind, body, and soul is essential. Get to know yourself better by taking short trips alone. Make dinner reservations for one. Take a dance or exercise class. Learn a new language. Visit a new art exhibit or volunteer for a cause close to your heart. Find a faith-based house of worship for spiritual renewal and growth. This may be difficult and uncomfortable, but it is necessary before starting a new relationship. Your emotions are fragile—just like mine were—and you need to surround yourself with an accountability village that will support you and share words of encouragement, tough love, and kind rebuke.

Think like a lion and move like a lion. Not one drop of your self-worth depends on someone else's acceptance of you. If you constantly try to prove your worth to someone, instead of just being yourself, then you have already disrespected your worth. No one can offend you unless you are easily offended. No one can hurt your feelings unless you not easily bruised. No one can gaslight you unless you are 'gaslight able'. Are you catching my point? Self-worth is based on your consent, not someone else's, because no one can make you feel inferior without your permission.

Lastly, there is no reason to keep tearing yourself down when God builds you up daily. Monitor your self-conversations, as they can quickly produce doubt, shame, and fear. During my divorce, I forgot my self-worth. I assure you that you will experience lapses of confidence and forget how wonderfully made you are. When you need a listening ear, some correction, and a word of encouragement, carefully find a trusted friend. It works! I followed my advice and shortened my heartache. At the same time, I became a better version of myself when I allowed myself to fall in love with my body, my mind, and my wounded soul. I gained godly strength that guarded my heart during the process.

Stand before the mirror again and fill yourself with kind and tender words of affirmation: *I am in love with myself. I love and accept who I am and who I am becoming. I am a survivor and a vessel full of love.* You may not feel comfortable stating any of these affirmations but repeat them daily until you begin to feel them throughout every atom in your body with the purest of love.

AFFIRMATIONS:

- God loves me unconditionally.
- I love myself unconditionally.
- I know that the pain will ease, and I will find joy in life again.
- I will love again.
- I am worthy of love.
- I am always loving.
- I am compassionate to myself.
- I am kind, and kind to myself.
- I am loved and lovable.
- I deserve love, and one day I will find it.
- My heart is healing.
- I send my former partner love, peace, and happiness.
- I fill my heart with what is essential and leave the rest behind.
- I am infinitely worthy of love.
- I lovingly accept all the love from me and my soulmate.
- I am an attractive person.
- I am compassionate toward myself and my heart.

SCRIPTURES:

- *"I praise you because I am fearfully and wonderfully made; your works are wonderful; I know that full well"* (Psalm 139:14, KJV).

- *"You were bought at a price"* (1 Corinthians 6:20, KJV).

- *"Even the hairs on your head are numbered. Do not be afraid; you are more valuable than many sparrows"* (Luke 12:7, KJV).

I believe forgiveness is the best form of love in any relationship. It takes a strong person to say they're sorry and an even stronger person to forgive.
— *Yolanda Hadid*

Promises

Resolving and determining may require a vow to oneself. Self-promises are made when you decide what is best for you physically, emotionally, and spiritually. Start this exercise by recording your declarations, decrees, and promises on the note pages. After documenting your thoughts, stand in front of the mirror and make these promises to yourself.

I hope you have become more comfortable looking at yourself in any mirror at this point as you recite the following pledges and affirmations to yourself:

AFFIRMATIONS:

- I promise to stay healthy by eating well and exercising regularly.
- I vow to find any reason to celebrate my life everyday.
- I pledge to connect with a group of friends who will encourage me to get healthy.
- I promise to seek good advice so that I do not make the same mistakes again.
- I promise to keep negativity out of my thoughts and mouth.
- I promise to embrace positivity.
- I promise to love who God has made me to be.
- I promise never to go to bed angry, even at myself.
- I promise to always put myself first.
- I promise to protect my heart and mind before I love again.
- I am working on myself, for myself.

SCRIPTURES:

- *"I can do all this through Him, who strengthens me"* (Philippians 4:13, KJV).

- *"The tongue has the power of life and death, and those who love it will eat its fruit"* (Proverbs 18:21, NIV).

- *"Trust in the Lord with all your heart; do not depend on your own understanding. Seek His will in all you do, and He will show you which path to take"* (Proverbs 3:5-6, NLT).

Only I can change my life. No one can do it for me.
— *Carol Burnett*

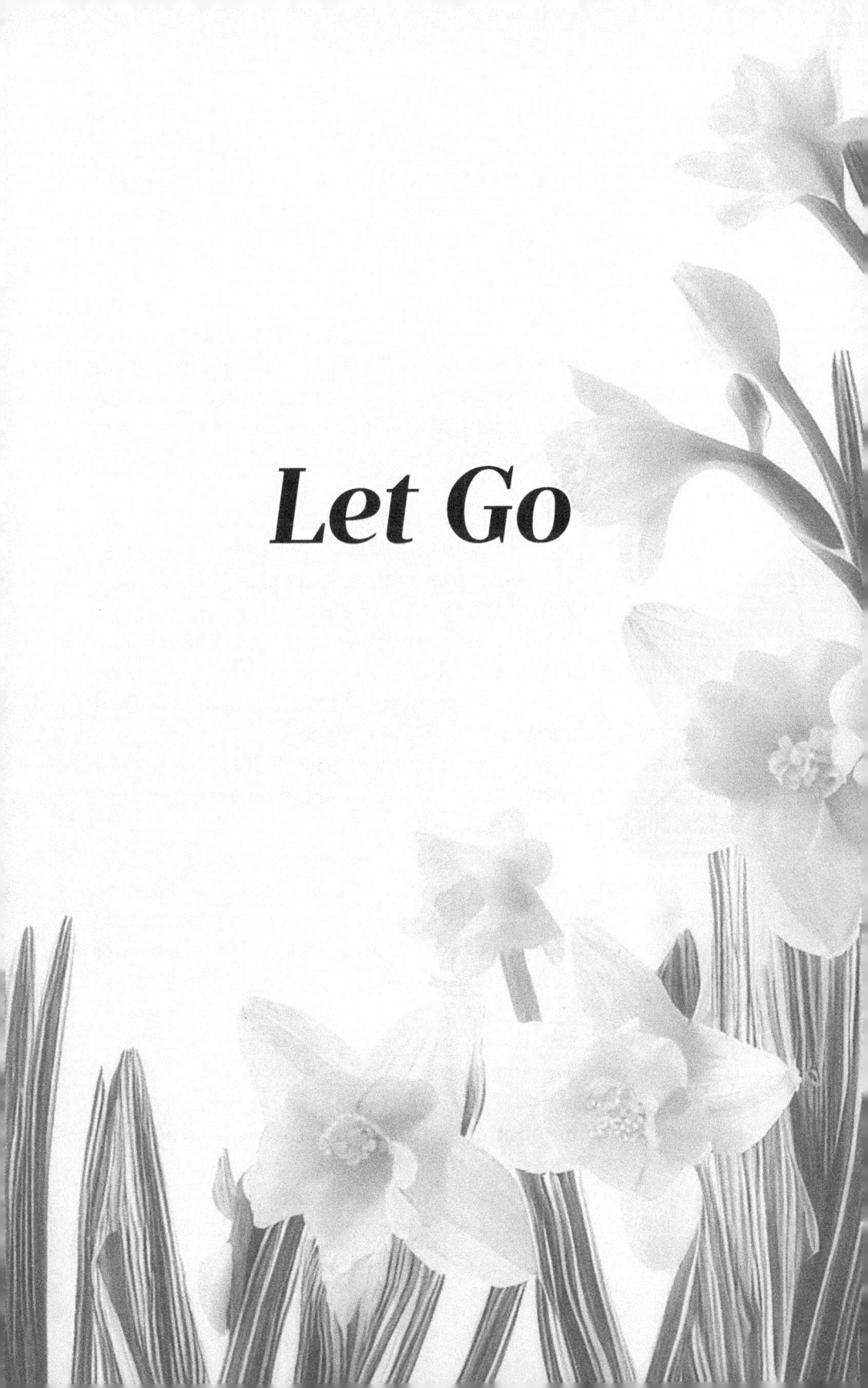

Let Go

I realized how burdened I was with emotional baggage. Some of my signs were internal, but I could not hide most of them. At that point, I knew I had to stop my fair share of "stinking thinking."

In 2000, American songwriter Erykah Badu released a powerful song called *Bag Lady*. These lyrics came to life for me, and I promised myself that I would never become a bag lady again. At some point, we all must ask ourselves, *Am I a bag lady?*

If you are unfamiliar with the benefits of Emotional House Cleaning (EHC), you may be burdened by tremendous emotional baggage from your marriage and divorce. I encourage you to take a minute to revisit the EHC process. However, if you are familiar with EHC in Chapter 1, I commend you for doing the work. Keeping it all inside will cause stress, and too much stress will kill you. Loneliness is an indication that you are in the wrong place. It is not a space you want to stay in for too long because loneliness breeds depression, and this can sometimes encourage destructive behaviors before you realize it.

Take a few minutes and identify three emotional bags or (triggers) you are carrying. It's time to be honest with yourself, let go of unhealthy habits, and prepare to move onto the road of emotional freedom. This is a big step. God knows that you are hurting, but remember He is near the brokenhearted, even more than you may realize. He feels your pain and confusion. Do not despair. God is with you.

I highly recommend that you seek help with your healing from two places—at the altar and on the couch of a licensed therapist. Start by meditating on the Word of God to rebuild your strength and find your way back to a place of wholeness. Do not be ashamed to reach out to a professional therapist. They can also be divine instruments of God.

AFFIRMATIONS:

- Everything is unfolding as it is supposed to.
- I am allowing myself to let go.
- I choose to be at peace with the way that things are.
- I promise to let everything good for me come to me.

I have sought and received godly advice wherever the Lord led me. To this day, I seek talk therapy and advice whenever I feel the need to talk through an issue.

Here are some Bible verses that mention wise counsel:

- *"For by wise counsel, you will wage your war, and in a multitude of counselors, there is safety"* (Proverbs 24:6, NKJV).

- *"The way of a fool is right in his own eyes: but he that hearkeneth unto counsel is wise"* (Proverbs 12:15, KJV).

- *"Hear counsel, and receive instruction, that thou mayest be wise in thy latter end"* (Proverbs 19:20, ASV).

- *"Plans are established by seeking advice; so if you wage war, obtain guidance."* (Proverbs 20:18, NIV).

Many of us can agree that wisdom is found in the counsel of many. I remind myself that I am not alone and that there is always someone who can help me through any situation with prayer. I surrounded myself with sincere friends who loved and encouraged me to overcome my heartache and grief. I was tired of crying over my failed marriage. My counselors' tribe was many, and they helped me regain my power. They also held me accountable for breaking cycles of depression and loneliness.

I spoke to anyone who would listen to me. I mean A-N-Y-O-N-E! The more I talked about my heartbreak, the better I felt. Let it out by any means necessary.

I quickly learned that I could not love again while carrying all the emotional baggage from my past into my future. Allow yourself to replace those negative emotions with thoughts of joy, peace, forgiveness, and acceptance. Let it go, my friend. You deserve better.

Tips to Overcome Divorce Stress:

1. Identify and accept your feelings.
2. Stop blaming yourself and others by taking responsibility.
3. Keep the focus on yourself.
4. Focus on your children (if applicable).
5. Learn a new activity and master it.
6. Try new things.
7. Get support.

> **"You can't defeat the darkness by keeping it caged inside of you."**
> — *Seth Adam Smith*

What's New and What's Next

Getting a divorce brings about more than a mixed bag of emotions. This process also forces many of us to make unwanted, unfamiliar, uncomfortable decisions quickly. Sometimes, these emotions can consume you while you are moving toward healing. Remember, you can find peace, clarity, joy, and self-love. If you experience disappointment, hurt, loneliness, confusion, and frustration, know that freedom awaits you on the other side of your healing.

Some of you may be battling suicidal thoughts, but hold on, dear brother and dear sister—there is hope and assistance around the corner. Never forget that you are not alone. You are not alone. But you must reach out to find resources designed to help you with your every need. Resources come in a variety of ways and you can readily find them in the palm of your hand. A trusted friend or family member comes to mind, housing, food, a safe haven, transportation, or a shoulder to cry on. A renewed purpose, a rebirth, and a new beginning await you. If you have this guidebook, your destiny already looks brighter and better. God's got you!

Here are a few positive effects that divorce can have on your new single life:

Positive Effects of Divorce:

- **Freedom and Independence**
  Divorce allows individuals to make choices and live on their own terms.

- **Personal Growth**
  Divorce can lead to self-discovery, self-love, and personal growth, increasing self-esteem and a stronger sense of self.

- **Improved Health**
  Divorce can lead to improved health, with increased self-confidence and less stress. This can foster a renewed drive to live healthier and improve overall well-being.

- **Sense of Self-Awareness**
  Divorce can help individuals realize how strong they are and develop coping skills. Talking to positive and accepting friends and family or working with a therapist can support self-reflection and help with coping.

- **Pursuing New Interests**
  Some individuals may explore new hobbies or travel to destinations they never considered while married. Divorce can empower people to take risks and embrace opportunities they might have avoided in the past.

- **Better Environment for Children**
  In some cases, divorce can protect children from abuse and provide an opportunity to rebuild broken families in a healthier environment.

SCRIPTURES:

- *"My soul, be at rest in God alone, from whom comes my hope"* (Psalms 62:5, NAB).

- *"For I know the plans I have for you,"* says the LORD. *"They are plans for good and not for disaster, to give you a future and a hope"* (Jeremiah 29:11, NLT).

- *"Do not fear (anything), for I am with you; Do not be afraid, for I am your God. I will strengthen you; be assured I will help you; I will certainly take hold of you with My righteous right hand (a hand of justice, of power, of victory, of salvation)"* (Isaiah 41:10, AMP).

"Rebuild and discover your true strength and worth."
— *Patricia Mullins*

Time to Heal

I am a huge advocate of the healing journey. I received a fair amount of good advice from great women who had their own war stories. The advice I received was to give myself time to grieve—be sad, angry, hurt, devastated, afraid, and THEN, I had to learn how to manage those self-destructive emotions by replacing them with healthy habits.

To help put me back on track, I would remind myself why I filed for a divorce in the first place. It is essential to quickly deal with all the underlying emotions during your divorce. When you operate from a place of clarity, love, and forgiveness, you will stop the blame game and allow the healing process to begin. You must also recognize when it's time to stop the negative talk about your partner. When you pray for love, grace, and wholeness for your ex-spouse, then you are on your way to healing. You will begin to see yourself growing emotionally stronger and spiritually wiser.

How long does it take to heal? The healing process can take months or even years. Only you can answer that. I recommend that you set a time to graduate from your process so you can move on from dysfunction and to adopt a new set of normalcy. Only you can determine when you are ready to move ahead. Ask God to shorten your heartache and grant you peace.

It is mirroring time again. With firm conviction, proclaim the following five affirmations:

AFFIRMATIONS:

- I am clothed and in my right mind.
- I release all toxic thoughts and habits.
- I will take it one day at a time.
- I believe that this, too, shall pass.

- I am growing into a healed person, ready to love again.

SCRIPTURE:

- *"He heals the brokenhearted and binds up their wounds"* (Psalm 147:3, NIV).

- *"He gives strength to the weary and increases the power of the weak"* (Isaiah 40:29, NIV).

- *"By His wounds you have been healed"* (1 Peter 2:24, NIV).

- *"So do not fear, for I am with you; do not be dismayed for I am your God. I will strengthen you and help you; I will uphold you with my righteous right hand"* (Isaiah 41:10, NIV).

- *"Love bears all things, believes all things, hopes all things, endures all things".* (1 Corinthians 13:7, NIV).

"You can't have one without the other, time and healing can be your best companions."
— *Patricia Mullins*

A Change
of Scenery

We can all agree that life is stressful and can come at you from all angles. A manual for an easy, stress-free divorce would be welcomed, but it does not exist. However, a change of scenery can help your recovery simply because your environment greatly affects your attitude. Relocating after a divorce can be beneficial for many reasons—even if it is just for a fresh start, which is often the main reason.

Have you thought about what is best for you? Do you have children to consider and the impact to their lives? If so, I am sure you may have considered changing your scenery. It's not a simple or easy decision by any means, but by moving to a new home (out of town or state) to gain a fresh start can be just what you need. For me, the decision was easy when I packed up and moved back to Florida, as there were no children to consider. After putting a plan in place, I started my withdrawal process. I do not proclaim that the plan will be simple for everyone, but a plan is essential for all and considering a change of scenery is one part of it. I recommend first starting with a series of questions that you will want to be honest with yourself about in this process. Start here.

Questions to Consider:

If you answer yes to any of the following questions, relocating might be a feasible option for you:

1. Am I constantly rehashing unhealthy emotions and actions about the home or the city I shared with my ex-spouse?

2. Was my environment filled with abusive experiences that caused me to feel unsafe, saddened, or lonely?

3. Will moving across or out of town bring peace of mind for my children and me?

4. Does a better support system await me elsewhere than I have now?

Sometimes, the memories of a broken relationship are more challenging to let go of than making the decision itself. Moving can feel frightening and paralyzing, but you can do it. Decide and write down a timeline for when you want to move. For some people, it is easier not to plan than to face the harsh reality that things will never change without creating an action plan for your next move.

Unfortunately, you can get stuck in a rut without even realizing it. Review the questions above until you experience a healthy sense of clarity and insight.

I remember how fearful I felt when I moved across town and, later, out of state. Both moves were equally daunting for me, but I had no regrets. Returning to my hometown provided me with a better support system. That move turned out to be the best decision I ever made for my general well-being. I did not know it at the time, but I was practicing steps to let go and discovering how brave I could be on my own.

For those navigating an uncontested divorce with no children or property, the process can often be resolved quickly. In all decisions, ask God to guide your every move. If there are no children involved and your split was simply a parting of ways, you may not need to notify your ex-spouse about your move. However, if you are still in the divorce process, you should notify your attorney (this is what I did before I moved out of state).

AFFIRMATIONS:

- I promise to practice new habits that promote a brighter and healthier me.
- Not a drop of my self-worth depends on anyone accepting me.
- I will never let my motivation to do well focus on proving myself to others. My inspiration is centered on Christ.
- I am ready to receive that love.

SCRIPTURES:

- *"Trust in the Lord with all your heart and lean not on your own understanding; in all your ways, acknowledge Him, and He will make your paths straight"* (Proverbs 3:5-6, KJV).

- *"When you pass through the waters, I will be with you; and through the rivers, they shall not overflow you. When you walk through the fire, you shall not be burned.... Since you were precious in my sight, you have been honored and I have loved you"* (Isaiah 43:2,4, KJV).

- *"Have I not commanded you? Be strong and courageous. Do not be terrified; do not be discouraged, for the Lord your God will be with you wherever you go"* (Joshua 1:9, KJV).

- *"Set your hearts on the things above. Set your minds on the things above, not on earthly things. Your life is now hidden with Christ in God"* (Colossians 3:1-3, KJV).

"Accept yourself and keep moving forward. If you want to fly, you have to give up what weighs you down."
— *Roy T. Bennett*

Watch Your Mouth

So, let us talk about watching the words that come from our mouths. I cannot tell you how often I spoke out of both sides of my mouth during my divorce. On certain days, I had good things to say, while on other days, I had nothing but negative remarks about my ex-spouse and the situation I was in because of this divorce. Both were centered on the failure of my marriage and the hurt I endured.

Here are thirteen valuable verses you can hide in your heart by memorizing—they can help you watch your words. You might ask yourself, why so many scriptures for such a short chapter. Because we need reminding, as often as posssible that LIFE AND DEATH lives behind our lips, between our gums and is hidden in the middle of our faces. Being that it is so easy to slip between speaking life to ourselves; to then speaking death, in a matter of seconds. Words are powerful and can be used for both good and evil. If you are like some of us, going through the tragic death of a relationship, you may have conversations—both in your head and spoken aloud—that can lead you down a path of bitterness.

Scriptures Ahead

SCRIPTURES:

1. *"Words from the mouth of the wise are gracious, but fools are consumed by their lips"* (Ecclesiastes 10:12, NIV).

2. *"Whoever loves life and sees good days must keep their tongue from evil and their lips from deceitful speech"* (1 Peter 3:10, NIV).

3. *"Those who consider themselves religious and yet do not keep a tight rein on their tongues deceive themselves, and their religion is worthless"* (James 1:26, NIV).

4. *"May these words of my mouth and this meditation of my heart be pleasing in your sight, LORD, my Rock, and my Redeemer"* (Psalm 19:14, NIV).

5. *"Let your conversation always be full of grace, seasoned with salt, so that you may know how to answer everyone"* (Colossians 4:6, NIV).

6. *"Do not let your mouth lead you into sin"* (Ecclesiastes 5:6, NIV).

7. *"Set a guard over my mouth, LORD; keep watch over the door of my lips"* (Psalm 141:3, NIV).

8. *"Do not let any unwholesome talk come out of your mouth, but only what is helpful for building others up according to their needs, that it may benefit those who listen"* (Ephesians 4:29, NIV).

9. *"Before a word is on my tongue, you, LORD, know it completely"* (Psalm 139:4, NIV).

10. *"Though you probe my heart, though you examine me at night and test me, you will find that I have planned no evil; my mouth has not transgressed"* (Psalm 17:3, NIV).

11. *"The words of a wise man's mouth are gracious and win him favor, but the lips of a fool consume him; the beginning of his talking is foolishness, and the end of his talk is wicked madness"* (Ecclesiastes 10:12-13, AMP).

12. *"Whoever desires to love life and see good days, let him keep his tongue from evil and his lips from speaking deceit"* (1 Peter 3:10, ESV).

13. *"Let your conversation be gracious and attractive so that you will have the right response for everyone"* (Colossians 4:6, NLT).

Be careful with your words. Once they are said, they can only be forgiven, not forgotten.
— Ella

Encouraging Prayers

When I got married, I never thought I would end up divorced. When it did happen, I wondered in disbelief—*Is this happening to me? Is divorce part of my story?* If your spouse chooses to divorce, you may feel utterly shocked, crushed, and betrayed. You are trying desperately to save your marriage, and you have agonized over the divorce decision. You carefully study Biblical grounds for divorce and seek wise counsel after years of praying and hoping for restoration. Divorce is painful, messy, and lonely, which-ever way you slice it. What God intended to last for a life-time is ending, bringing devastating loss and leaving us to face an unknown future with a heart full of hurt. Your world may turn upside down, but dear brother or sister, God sees and cares about you. He has comfort, hope, and wisdom to share in His Word and invites you to speak to Him. Consider this: bring all your questions, cares, and concerns to Him in prayer. He knows what you need and will guide you as you seek Him.

In my search for comfort during my divorce, I discovered prayers and affirmations that comforted me and trans-formed my perspective.

Here are eight prayers you can pray when facing a divorce.

> *"For the mountains may move and the hills disappear, but my faithful love for you will remain even then. My covenant of blessing will never be broken," says the LORD, who has mercy on you* (Isaiah 54:10, NLT).

Lord, I thank You for Your love. The love I had hoped for in my marriage has disappointed and broken me. It is a pain that runs deep. But I can turn to You and trust Your unwavering, faithful love. You are the One who will never break Your promises to me. Your mercy is greater than my sins. In Christ, I am free from failure, flaw, or faithlessness that can separate us. Please give me stability and comfort in Your love. Remind me that this is who I am because of Jesus. I am Yours.

> *"For the house of Israel and the house of Judah have been utterly unfaithful to Me," declares the LORD* (Jeremiah 5:11, NLT).

God, I feel alone and wholly rejected! I gave my heart and myself to this person. How can they so easily walk away? Do I mean so little to them? You understand the betrayal and pain I am walking through. The people have repeatedly rejected You, yet You have loved perfectly. Please comfort me. Please show me what to do. I am still trying to figure out how to move forward. Let this experience draw me closer to Your heart so I can know You better. You will always be faithful.

> *"I weep with sorrow; encourage me by Your Word. Keep me from lying to myself, give me the privilege of knowing Your instructions"* (Psalm 119:28-29, NLT).

Father, I cannot stop crying. My emotions are right underneath the surface, constantly ready to spill out. My mind can barely think of anything besides grief and pain. It is hard to focus on Your Word, but I desperately need to hear from You. There are so many lies I am tempted to believe right now about You, me, and my situation. Meet me in this place and teach me what is true. Show me what You see. Please lead me to scriptures that encourage, guide, and give me hope.

> *"God was in Christ, reconciling the world to Himself, no longer counting people's sins against them, and*

He gave us this wonderful message of reconciliation"
(2 Corinthians 5:19, NLT).

God, when my relationship with You was broken because of sin, You sent Christ to the cross. You did everything needed to bring me back to You. Thank You, Lord! Your power and love have redeemed my life. I know You can bring reconciliation in the most seemingly hopeless situations, and I long to see my marriage restored. If it is Your will, God, You can reconcile us to You and one another. I pray You will do it! Reconcile us for Your glory. Use our story to display Your power to redeem.

"Search me, O God, and know my heart; test me and know my anxious thoughts. Point out anything in me that offends You and lead me along the path of everlasting life" (Psalm 139:23-24, NLT).

God, I confess that my defenses are up. I am hurt and angry. Pointing the finger at my spouse and focusing on how they have sinned against me is easy. But it feels scary to think about my sin now that divorce is on the table. I fear admitting failures as if I would accept the blame for losing our marriage. Remind me that whatever sins are in my heart, You have mercy for me in Christ. You are my refuge, a safe place to be honest and examine my heart. Show me where I have turned from trusting and following You. Lead me in Your wisdom, gentleness, and love. Show me how to walk with You in righteousness.

"I am exhausted and completely crushed. My groans come from an anguished heart. You know what I long for, Lord; You hear my every sigh" (Psalm 38:8-9, NLT).

Lord, I am weary and so broken. Be merciful to me! Please look at my distress and come close to me. Hear my prayers and requests. Sometimes, I feel like You are not listening, but I know You see my heart. You know my unmet desires, my broken dreams, and my fears. You are with me in my pain, even when I am a mess. I need Your comfort and healing. Reassure me of Your love now and bring me peace.

> *"He will not crush the weakest reed or put out a flickering candle. He will bring justice to all who have been wronged"* (Isaiah 42:3, NLT).

Jesus, You are mighty but gentle. You have compassion for the weak and oppressed. This divorce has brought me so low, and I am spent. I cannot handle much more. Hold me up in Your strength. You see how I have been mistreated. Please fight for me. Help me to rest in You, trusting that You will make things right in Your wisdom at the right time. I know You love me. You gave Your life for me. I surrender and trust my life to You. You are the One who will take care of me.

> *"I still belong to You; You hold my right hand. You guide me with Your counsel, leading me to a glorious destiny"* (Psalm 73:23-24, NLT).

Lord, I have doubted; I have wrestled. I have been angry and questioned why You allow such brokenness in my marriage and family. I have struggled to understand, but You repeatedly bring me back to You. When I remember Your grace that saves me from destruction and gives me eternal life, I can see my present circumstances differently. This brokenness is not my forever story. You are still leading me home to You, to glory. I am still Yours, and You are still by my side. You will show me the way forward. Please help me to walk on in this hope. You have been good to me, and You always will be.

In closing, I pray these prayers will do the same for you, igniting a spark of hope and leading you toward spiritual growth and freedom.

REFERENCES

Bothell Christian Counseling. "What to Do When You Feel Stuck in an Unhappy Marriage" https://bothellcounseling.com/what-to-do-when-you-feel-stuck-in-an-unhappy-marriage-2/

Boose, Paul. "Forgiveness does not change the past, but it does enlarge the future."

Tampa Counseling Place: https://tampacounselingplace.com/divorced/

The Holy Bible

ONLINE RESOURCES

www.peaceafterdivorce.com

www.christiancollectiveministry.com

www.womensdivorce.com

www.menliving.org

www.marriage.com

www.dc4k.org

www.mensgroup.com

www.nacsdc.org

www.safepacefl.org

www.bible.com

ABOUT PATRICIA

Patricia A. Mullins is a vessel of infinite optimism, hope, and faith. She serves her community as an educator, entrepreneur, and serial encourager. Patricia aims to equip others globally who are or have been suffering from the stress associated with divorce.

Students are a big part of Patt's mission. Both known, and highly respected for her direct yet light-hearted approach to teaching, mentoring, and coaching others to achieve positive outcomes. She makes quite an impact in many circles.

Patricia lives in South Florida, where she enjoys her singlehood by using the ten steps she discovered and implemented.

Grateful for the opportunity to speak at organizations, academia, and faith-based groups, Patricia selfishly works at finding her better self with the ten steps in this book. Passionate about empowering divorcees who desire to be healed, this guidebook was conceived out of Patricia's need to find LIGHT in a dark place. Armed with these tools, she continues to practice daily mental, emotional, spiritual, and physical renewal.

Contact Patricia at: iampatriciamullins@gmail.com

_____
_____
_____
_____
_____
_____
_____
_____
_____
_____
_____
_____
_____
_____
_____
_____
_____
_____
_____
_____
_____
_____
_____
_____

_____

_____

_____

_____

_____

_____

_____

_____

_____

_____

_____

_____

_____

_____

_____

_____

_____

_____

_____

_____

_____

_____